Tabernacle Classics

25
GREAT SOUTHERN GOSPEL FAVORITES

ARRANGED FOR CHOIR BY
MOSIE LISTER

Lillenas PUBLISHING COMPANY

Kansas City, MO 64141

The "Oasis" Choir
(O.A.S.I.S)

CONTENTS

OLDER Adults Still iN SERVICE

	Choral Edition	Solo Edition
Canaanland Is Just in Sight	4	2
I Thirst	9	8
Keep on the Firing Line	13	12
Led by the Master's Hand	18	17
I'm Not Giving Up	22	21
The Broken Rose	26	25
Your First Day in Heaven	30	29
His Grace Is Sufficient for Me	34	33
New Shoes	39	38
I Will Serve Thee	44	44
I Never Shall Forget the Day	46	47
Beyond the Cross	49	50
Down on My Knees	53	55
I Should Have Been Crucified	57	60
Do You Know My Jesus?	60	63
The Unclouded Day	64	68
I Bowed on My Knees and Cried, "Holy!"	69	74
Ride That Chariot	75	81
Love Is Why	80	85
Love Was in the Room	83	88
A Storm Now and Then	86	91
The Meeting in the Air	91	95
Faith Unlocks the Door	97	101
Joy Comes in the Morning	100	104
Peace in the Midst of the Storm	104	108

Song begins on page 2 in the Solo/Accompaniment Edition

Canaanland Is Just in Sight

Words and Music by
JEFF GIBSON
Arr. by Mosie Lister

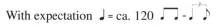

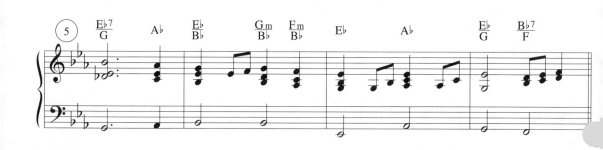

2 part choir
Ladies unison

Mo - ses led God's chil - dren, for - ty years He led them

Men unison

Through the cold and through the night.

Divisi

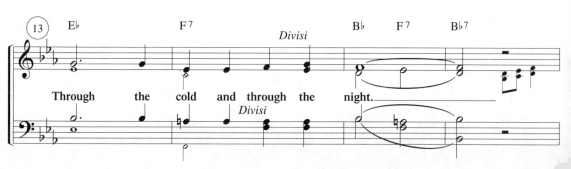

4

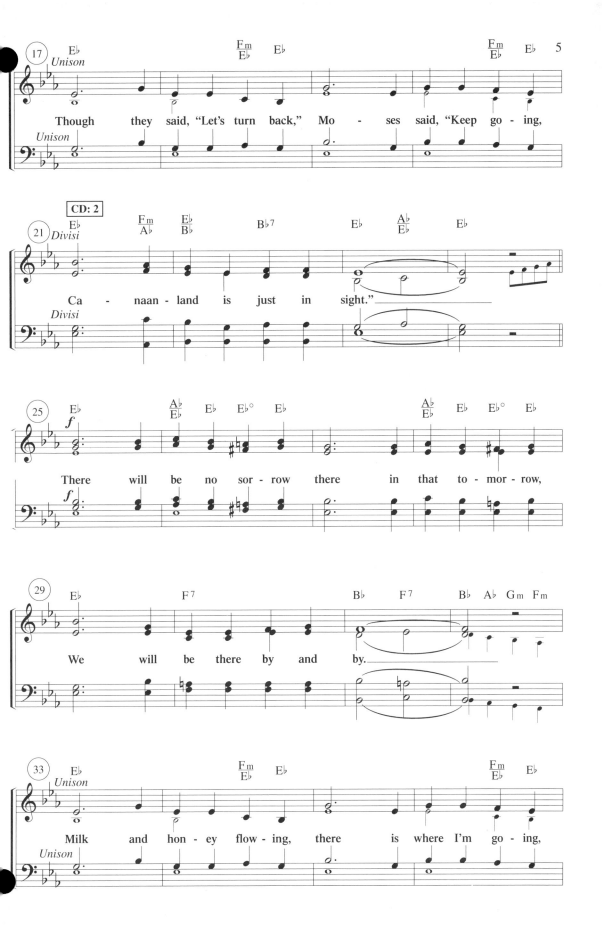

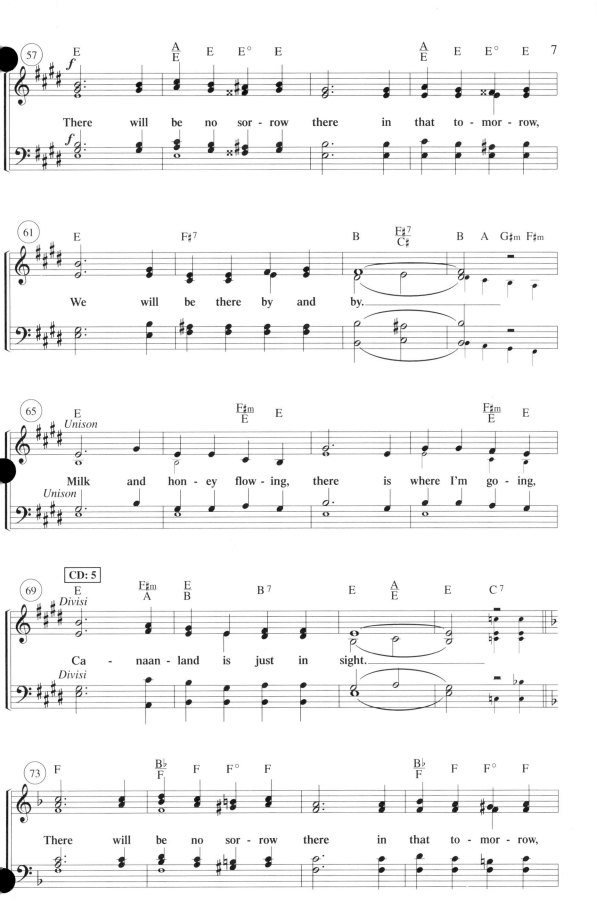

We will be there by and by.

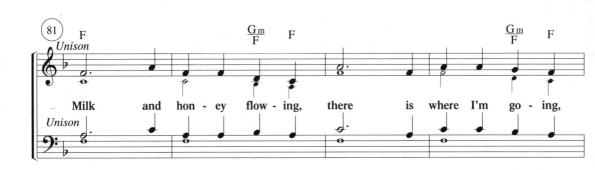

Milk and hon - ey flow - ing, there is where I'm go - ing,

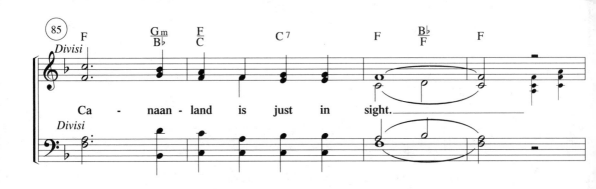

Ca - naan - land is just in sight.

Ca - naan - land is just in sight.

(10)

I Thirst

Words and Music by
BEN LOWRY
Arr. by Mosie Lister

10

He gave me wa-ter that I had nev-er dreamed of, But for this wa-ter my Lord had to die. He said, "I He said, "I thirst," ____ yet He made the riv-ers. He said, "I thirst," yet He made the sea.

Keep on the Firing Line

Unknown
Arr. by Mosie Lister

Song begins on page 17 in the Solo/Accompaniment Edition

Led By the Master's Hand

Words and Music by
MOSIE LISTER
Arr. by Mosie Lister

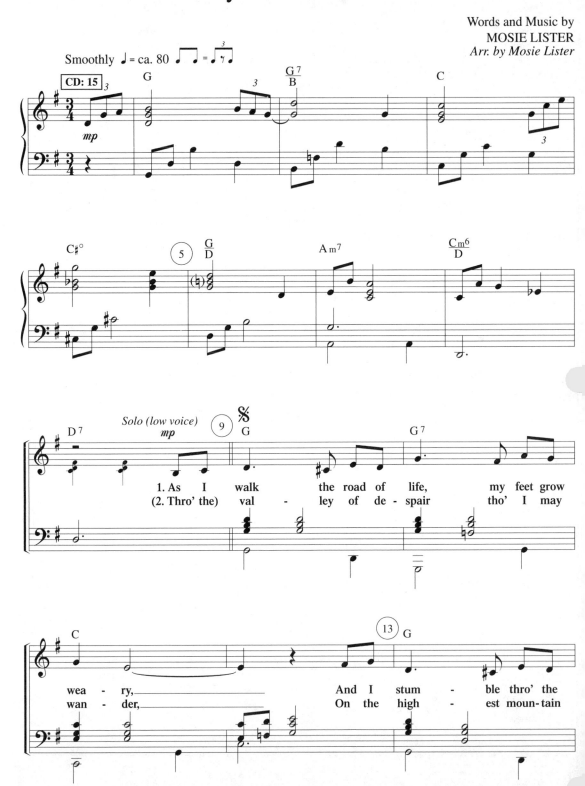

Song begins on page 21 in the Solo/Accompaniment Edition

I'm Not Giving Up

Words and Music by
SQUIRE E. PARSONS, JR.
Arr. by Mosie Lister

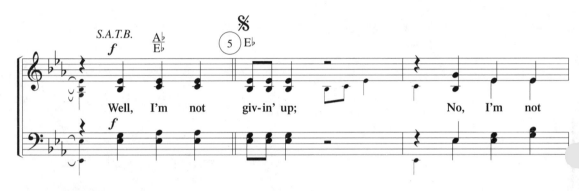

The Broken Rose

Words and Music by
SQUIRE E. PARSONS JR.
Arr. by Mosie Lister

1. Words can - not de - scribe its beau - ty as up -
(2. Then they) laid that Bro - ken Rose _____

on the stem it grows. ᭦ Match - less in its
in a bor - rowed tomb; But on the third _____

glo - ry, the ten - der lit - tle rose. When its
day _____ that Rose a - gain did bloom. Now _____

way. For - sak - en by His friends,

bruised by His foes, How sweet is the

CD: 26

fra - grance of heav - en's sweet Rose.

D.S. al Coda ⊕ CODA
(to pg. 26, meas. 6)
Men join sop.

2. Then they dwells. The most

beau - ti - ful Rose was bro - ken one

Song begins on page 29 in the Solo/Accompaniment Edition

Your First Day in Heaven

Words and Music by
STUART HAMBLEN
Arr. by Mosie Lister

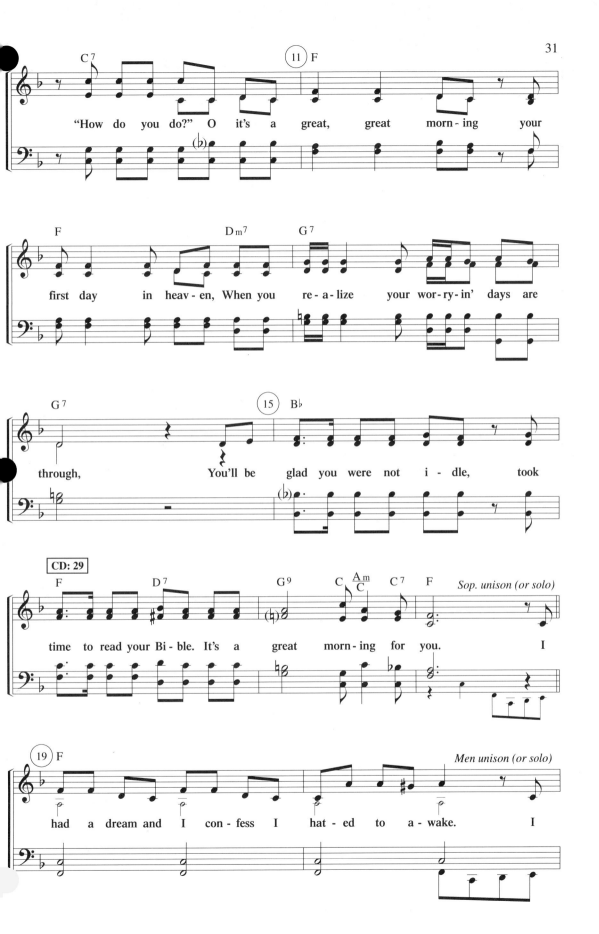

Song begins on page 33 in the Solo/Accompaniment Edition

His Grace Is Sufficient for Me

Words and Music by
MOSIE LISTER
Arr. by Mosie Lister

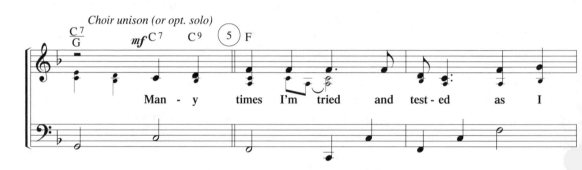

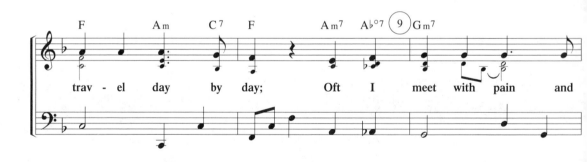

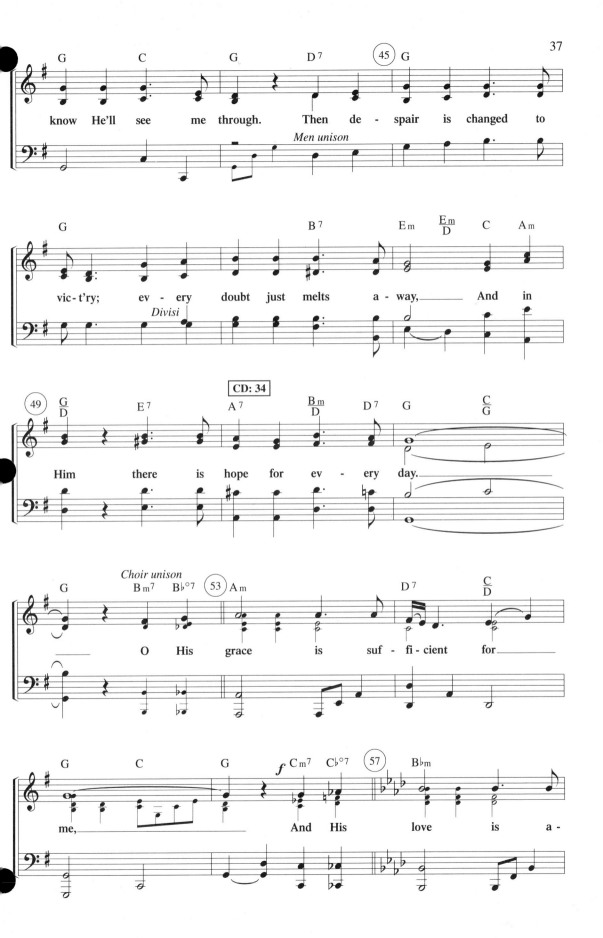

38

New Shoes

Words and Music by
MOSIE LISTER
Arr. by Mosie Lister

leads___ me,___ wher - ev - er that may be, And I'll

CD: 36

tell the world__ that Je - sus saves. The Book says

put on the ar - mor of the Lord___ With the shield of faith be - for

Optional unison

___ you, The Word of the liv-ing God___ your on - ly sword.___

___ Let_ your feet be shod with the gos - pel Of peace and un - der -

CD: 37

stand - ing, And go to all the world and preach His word.

And so in God's own pow'r that o - ver - comes The dev - il's flam - ing ar - rows, I go with my tongue made free to speak His Word, And I thank Him for these new shoes That take me where He

Song begins on page 44 in the Solo/Accompaniment Edition

I Will Serve Thee

WILLIAM J. GAITHER
and GLORIA GAITHER

WILLIAM J. GAITHER
Arr. by Mosie Lister

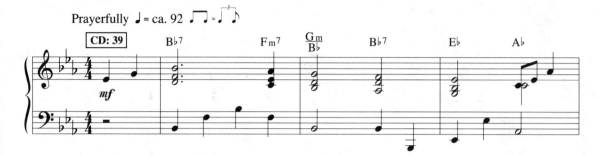

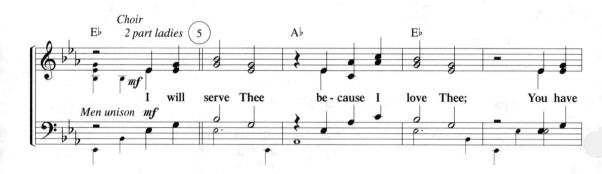

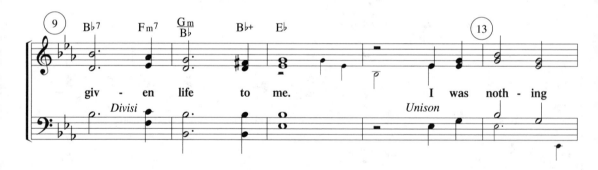

Song begins on page 47 in the Solo/Accompaniment Edition

I Never Shall Forget the Day

Words and Music by
G. T. SPEER
Arr. by Mosie Lister

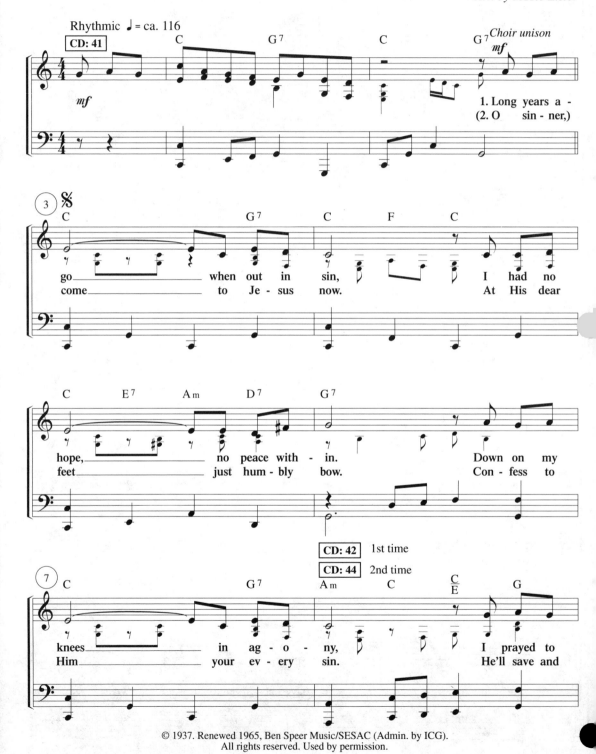

Beyond the Cross

Words and Music by
MOSIE LISTER
Arr. by Mosie Lister

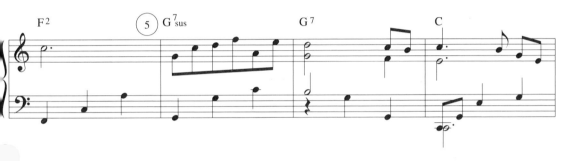

Need-ing strength for my jour-ney, I knelt at the

cross Where Je-sus once died for me,_____

Down On My Knees

Words and Music by
MOSIE LISTER
Arr. by Mosie Lister

CD: 51

D.S. al Coda (to pg. 53, meas. 5)

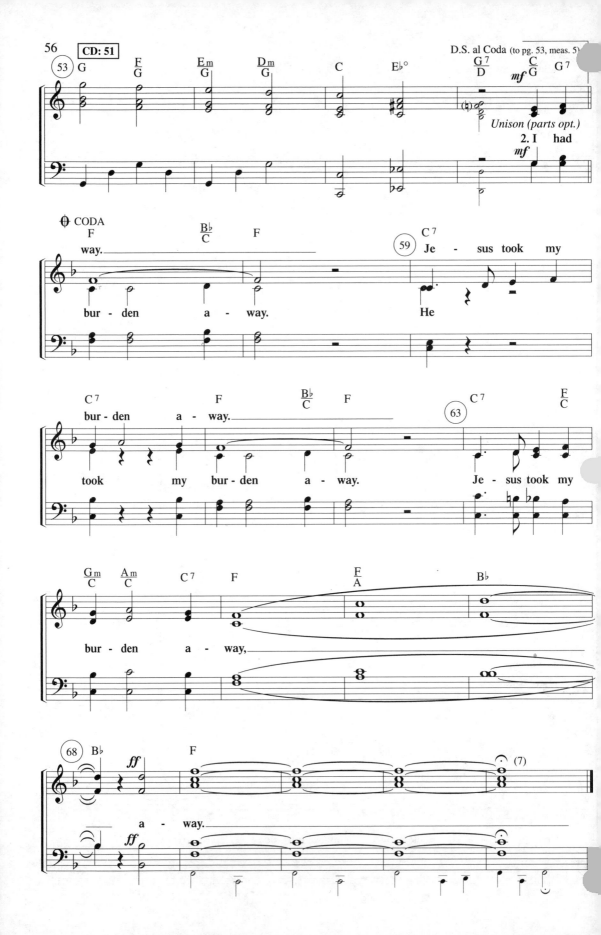

I Should Have Been Crucified

Words and Music by
GORDON JENSEN
Arr. by Mosie Lister

Song begins on page 63 in the Solo/Accompaniment Edition

Do You Know My Jesus?

Words and Music by
W. F. (Bill) LAKEY and
V. B. (Vep) ELLIS
Arr. by Mosie Lister

Have you a heart that's wea—ry, Tend—ing a

load of care?_____ Are you a

Song begins on page 68 in the Solo/Accompaniment Edition

The Unclouded Day

Words and Music by
REV. J. K. ALWOOD
Arr. by Mosie Lister

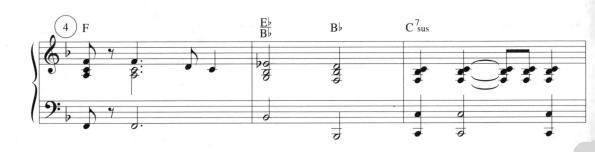

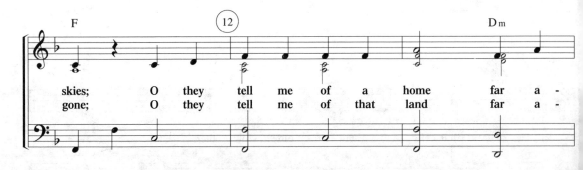

Song begins on page 74 in the Solo/Accompaniment Edition

I Bowed on My Knees and Cried, "Holy!"

Anonymous

E. M. DUDLEY CANTWELL
Arr. by Mosie Lister

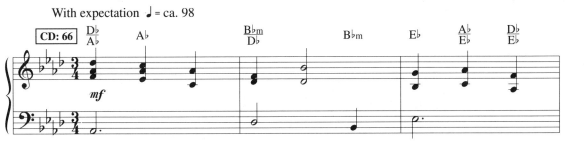

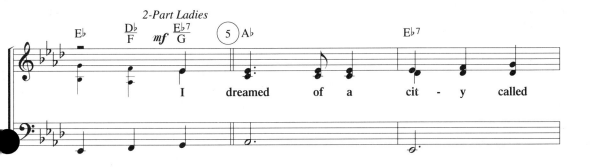

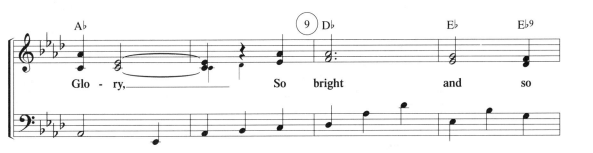

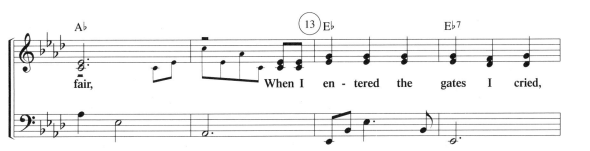

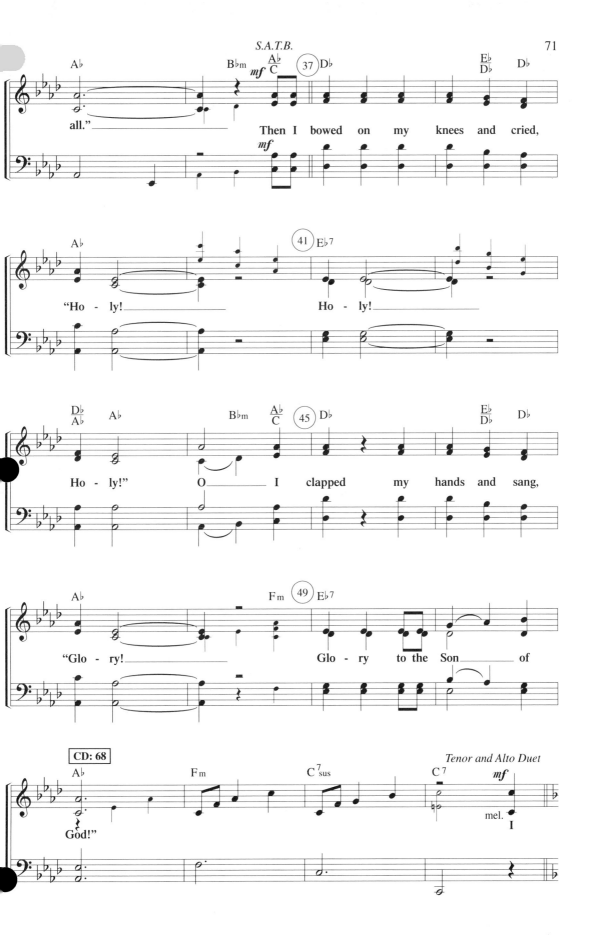

72

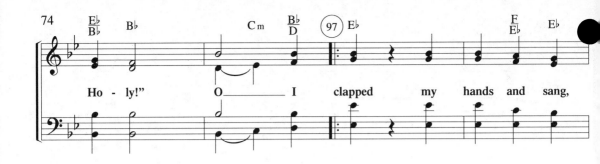

Ho - ly!"   O_____ I   clapped   my   hands   and   sang,

"Glo - ry!_____   Glo - ry   to   the   Son_____ of

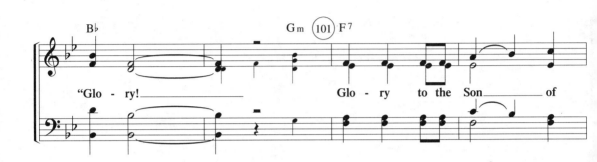

God!"   I   God!

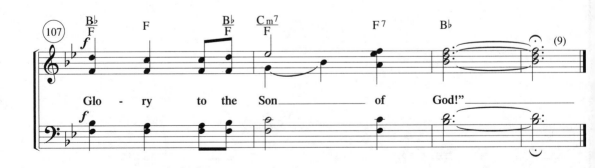

Glo - ry   to   the   Son_____ of   God!"_____

Ride That Chariot

Words and Music by
MOSIE LISTER
Arr. by Mosie Lister

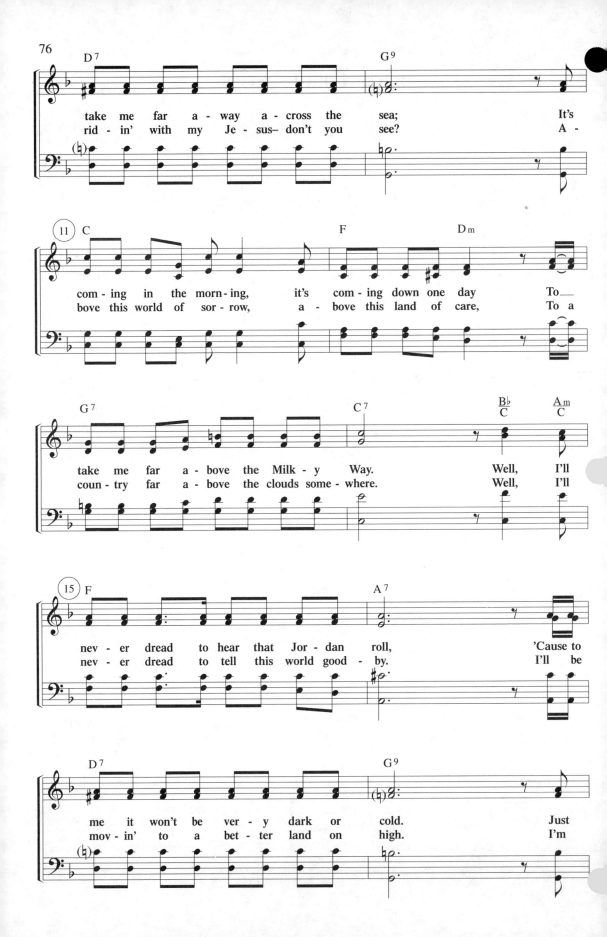

CD: 71 1st time
CD: 73 2nd time

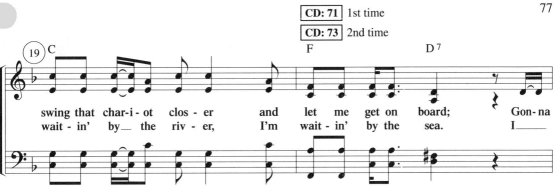

19 C   F   D7

swing that char-i-ot clos-er   and let me get on board;   Gon-na
wait-in' by the riv-er,   I'm wait-in' by the sea.   I

G9   C7   F

ride   that char-i-ot with my Lord.
know   it's com-in' af-ter me.

I'm gon-na

23 D7

Ride   that char-i-ot,   ride   that char-i-ot;

ride   that char-i-ot, gon-na ride it home some day.

G7

Ride   that char-i-ot,   ride   that char-i-ot;

Ride it home to Heav-en, gon-na ride it home to stay.

Ride that char-i-ot, ride that char-i-ot;
Soon they're gon-na be com - in', gon-na come right down af - ter me.

What a jub - i - lee!
What a glad hap - py morn-ing! What a jub - i - lee!_____ I'm gon - na

Ride that char-i-ot, ride that char-i-ot;
stand here look-in' and watch - in' 'til I see it com - in' down,

Ride that char-i-ot, ride that char-i-ot;
Keep my eyes on Heav - en 'til I leave this earth - ly ground.

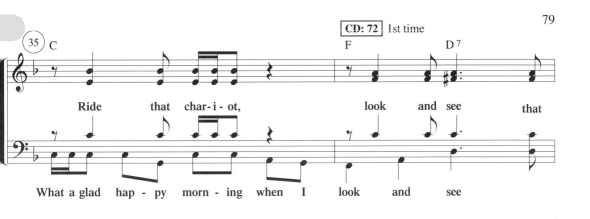

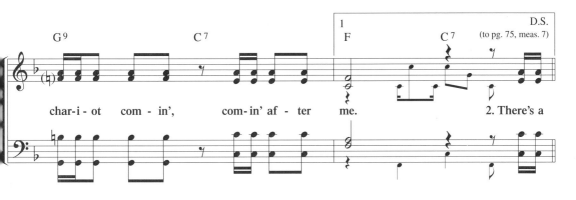

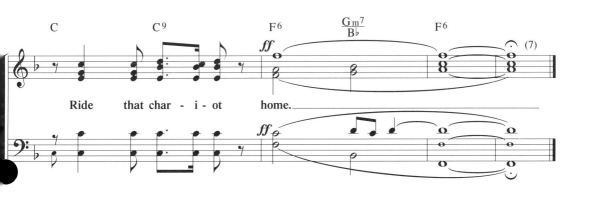

Song begins on page 85 in the Solo/Accompaniment Edition

Love Is Why

W. F. (Bill) LAKEY and
V. B. (Vep) ELLIS

DAVID ELLIS and
V. B. (Vep) ELLIS
Arr. by Mosie Lister

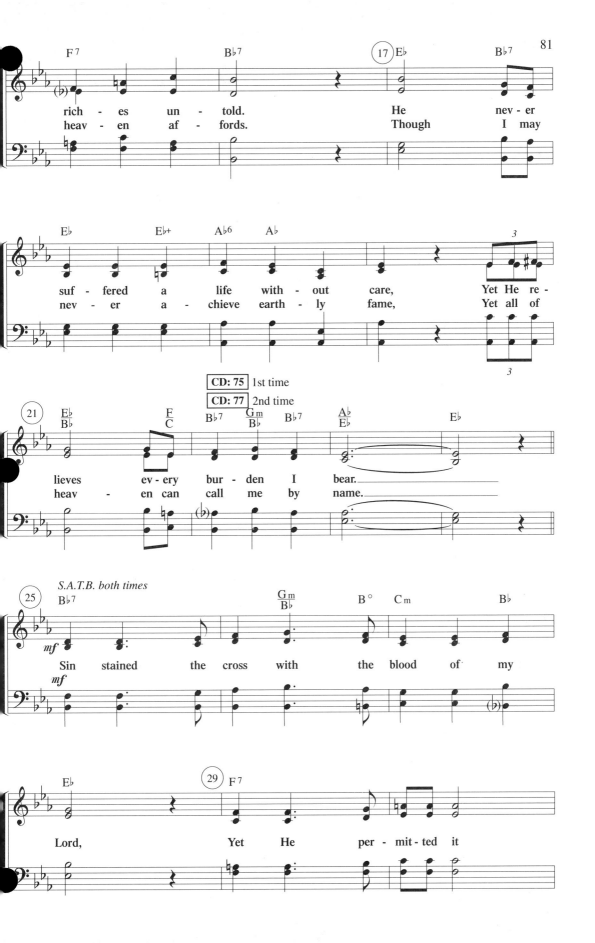

Love Was in the Room

KEN BIBLE and
MOSIE LISTER

MOSIE LISTER
Arr. by Mosie Lister

death and hell would nev-er reign a-gain. When the

glo-ry of the Liv-ing God____ broke through to the dark-ness of the

tomb, The earth was filled with His beau-ty, and love was in the

room. 2. I was room. The earth was

filled with His beau-ty, and love was in the room.____

Song begins on page 91 in the Solo/Accompaniment Edition

A Storm Now and Then

Words and Music by
MOSIE LISTER
Arr. by Mosie Lister

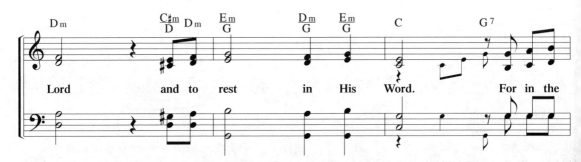

wind_____ and the rain I learned to call_____ on His

name. And I thank Him in my song; It took the

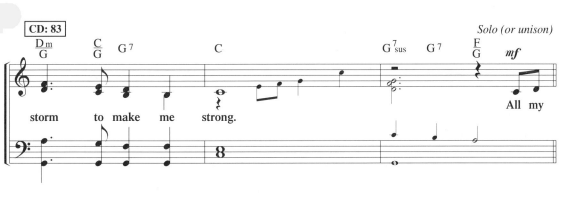

CD: 83

Solo (or unison)

storm to make me strong. All my

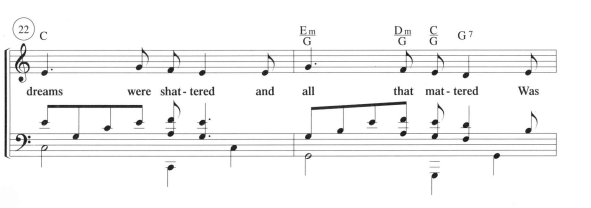

dreams were shat-tered and all that mat-tered Was

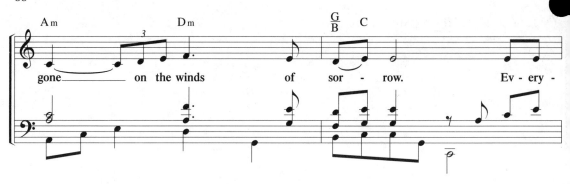

gone_____ on the winds of sor - row. Ev - ery -

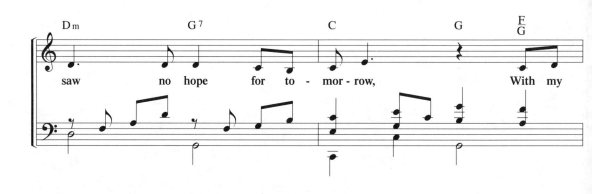

thing_____ I had planned swept out_____ of my hand, And I

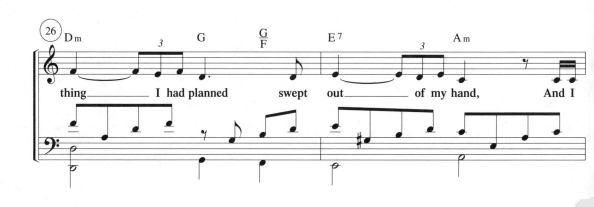

saw no hope for to - mor - row, With my

heart near to break - ing_____ I cried, "Lord,_____ I can't make it. By my-

Word. For in the wind_____ and the rain I learned to

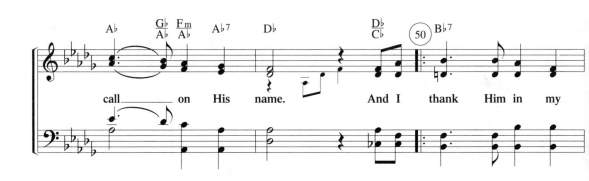

call_____ on His name. And I thank Him in my

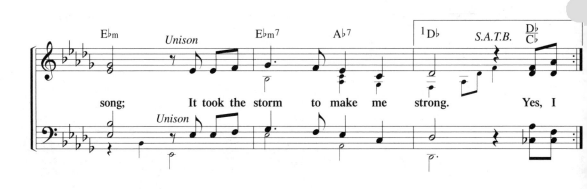

song; It took the storm to make me strong. Yes, I

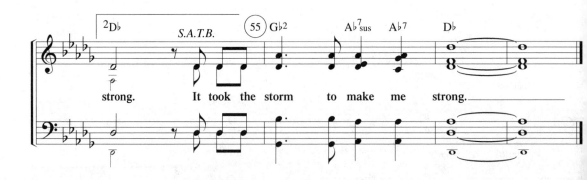

strong. It took the storm to make me strong._____

Song begins on page 95 in the Solo/Accompaniment Edition

The Meeting in the Air

Words and Music by
MAE TAYLOR ROBERTS
Arr. by Mosie Lister

CD: 87

Faith Unlocks the Door

Words and Music by
SAMUEL T. SCOTT and
ROBERT L. SANDS
Arr. by Mosie Lister

*Trust in the Lord with all your heart and lean not on your
own understanding; in all your ways acknowledge him,
and He will make your paths straight (Prov. 3:5-6, NIV**)

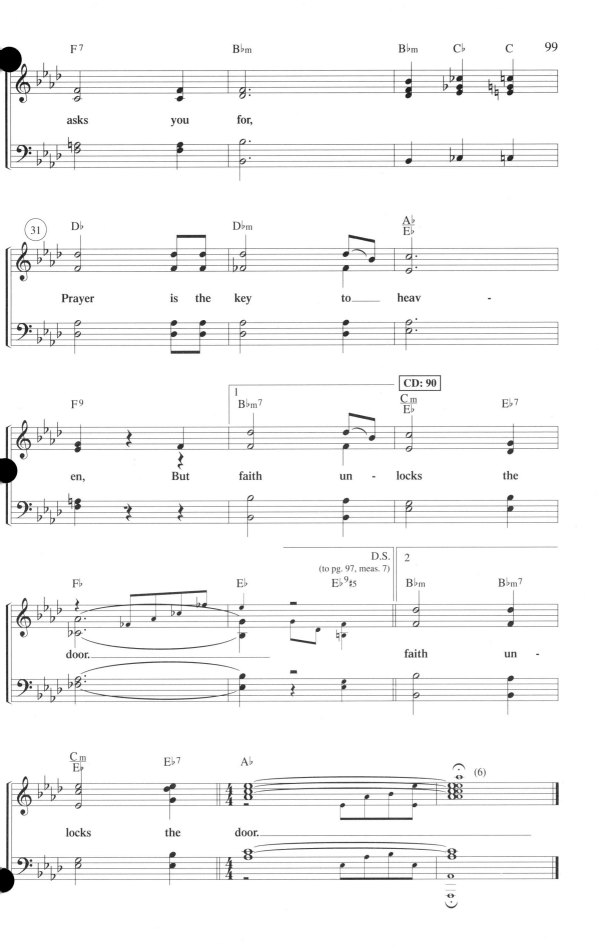

Song begins on page 104 in the Solo/Accompaniment Edition

Joy Comes in the Morning

WILLIAM J. GAITHER and
GLORIA GAITHER

WILLIAM J. GAITHER
Arr. by Mosie Lister

Song begins on page 108 in the Solo/Accompaniment Edition

Peace in the Midst of the Storm

Words and Music by
STEPHEN R. ADAMS
Arr. by Mosie Lister

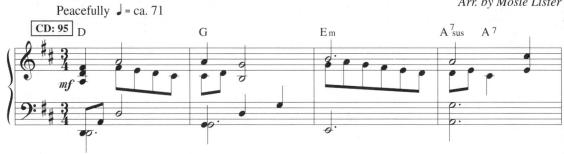

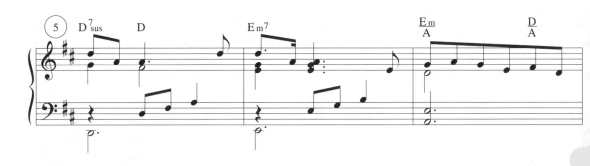

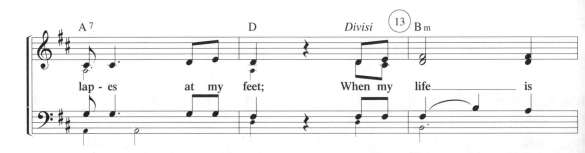

106